Date: 2/15/12

Animals

Mammals, Birds, Reptiles, Amphibians, Fish, and Other Animals

By
Shar Levine
Leslie Johnstone

Crabtree Publishing Company

www.crabtreebooks.com

Crabtree Publishing Company

www.crabtreebooks.com

Authors: Shar Levine, Leslie Johnstone
Series consultant: Sally Morgan, MA, MSc, MIBiol
Project director: Ruth Owen
Designer: Alix Wood
Editors: Mark Sachner, Adrianna Morganelli
Proofreader: Crystal Sikkens
Project manager: Kathy Middleton
Production coordinator: Katherine Berti
Prepress technician: Katherine Berti

Developed & Created by Ruby Tuesday Books Ltd

Front cover: An Atlantic Puffin—Birds are members of the
class Aves and are the most successful vertebrates
adapted to life in the air.

Title page: A female orangutan with her baby

Photographs:
Alamy: page 33
FLPA: pages 4 (top and bottom), 7, 9, 10 (bottom), 13, 16, 18 (right),
20, 21 (left and right), 23 (row three left), 24, 25, 26, 30, 31 (main),
32 (left and right), 36, 37 (bottom), 39, 40, 41 (top and bottom),
42 (left and right), 43
Getty Images: page 18 (left)
Robert Myers: page 27
Ruby Tuesday Books Ltd: page 10 (top)
Science Photo Library: pages 11, 14, 15, 17 (top, inset),
28 (left and right), 37 (top)
Seapics.com: David Shen: page 29
Shutterstock: front cover, pages 1, 8 (top all), 17 (main), 19,
23 (all excepting row three left), 27 (top), 31 (inset), 35, 38 (all)

Library and Archives Canada Cataloguing in Publication

Levine, Shar, 1953-
Animals : mammals, birds, reptiles, amphibians, fish,
and other animals / Shar Levine and Leslie Johnstone.

(A class of their own)
Includes index.
ISBN 978-0-7787-5372-8 (bound).--ISBN 978-0-7787-5386-5 (pbk.)

1. Animals--Classification--Juvenile literature.
2. Animals--Juvenile literature. I. Johnstone, Leslie
II. Title. III. Series: Class of their own

QL351.L49 2010   j590.1'2   C2009-907430-3

Library of Congress Cataloging-in-Publication Data

Levine, Shar, 1953-
Animals : mammals, birds, reptiles, amphibians, fish, and other animals / by
Shar Levine and Leslie Johnstone.
p. cm. -- (A class of their own)
Includes index.
ISBN 978-0-7787-5386-5 (pbk. : alk. paper) -- ISBN 978-0-7787-5372-8
(reinforced library binding : alk. paper)
1. Animals--Juvenile literature. I. Johnstone, Leslie. II. Title. III. Series.

QL49.L3857 2010
590.1'2--dc22
                                                                    2009051341

Crabtree Publishing Company

www.crabtreebooks.com   1-800-387-7650

Printed in the U.S.A./012010/BG20091216

Published in Canada
Crabtree Publishing
616 Welland Ave.
St. Catharines, Ontario
L2M 5V6

Published in the United States
Crabtree Publishing
PMB 59051
350 Fifth Avenue, 59th Floor
New York, New York 10118

Published in the United Kingdom
Crabtree Publishing
Maritime House
Basin Road North, Hove
BN41 1WR

Published in Australia
Crabtree Publishing
386 Mt. Alexander Rd.
Ascot Vale (Melbourne)
VIC 3032

Contents

WHAT ARE ANIMALS?

From the smallest known insects—so tiny that they cannot be viewed without the help of a microscope—to the world's largest animal, the blue whale, animals are perhaps the best known and most interesting group of living things to most of us. This is partly, of course, because as humans we are ourselves members of the animal kingdom!

What Makes All of Us Animals?

The simple answer is, a lot of things. For one, all animals eat other living things in order to survive. Almost all animals are made up of several cells, and those cells work together. In addition, all animals, from worms, insects, and fish to cats, dogs, and armadillos, are at some point in their life cycle able to move around independently.

CASE STUDY

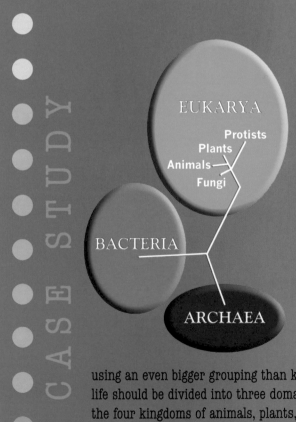

Kingdom or Domain?

The way life-forms are grouped, or classified, is constantly changing. Traditionally, organisms were classified as either animal or plant. Over the years, many organisms have been grouped *alongside* animals and plants, rather than *within* those two groups. For years, the classification of living things has been based on six *kingdoms* of life—animals, plants, fungi, protists, bacteria, and archaea.

As scientists improve their understanding of the genetic makeup of living things, they can better compare organisms. This understanding has helped scientists figure out even more detailed groupings of living things. In the past, organisms were grouped according to their appearance. Appearances can be misleading, however. Two organisms may look similar, but their genetic makeup can be very different. For example, some yeasts might be taken for bacteria based on the fact that, like bacteria, they consist of a single round cell. Today, yeasts are known to be fungi, not bacteria.

Some scientists now believe that organisms should be classified using an even bigger grouping than kingdom. This level is called the *domain*. These scientists propose that life should be divided into three domains—Eukarya, Bacteria, and Archaea. Within the domain Eukarya are the four kingdoms of animals, plants, fungi, and protists.

These kingdoms are more closely related to each other than to the domains of bacteria and archaea.

This is where things stand—for now. As scientists continue to make new discoveries, this system will undoubtedly turn out to be another chapter in the story of life!

All animals have bodies with parts that function together to allow the animals to grow and develop, produce offspring, and adjust to changes in the world around them. Animals have different ways to obtain and process their food, but all animals must eat and digest. Some animals can reproduce by themselves, while others need a mate, but all animals have offspring. Certain animals have very developed senses and are able to adapt readily to changes in their environments. Others lack a nervous system, but they are still able to change in response to changes in the world around them.

Many animals take part in rituals to secure a mate or reinforce a partnership. Here, a male blue-footed booby dances for his mate, showing her his feet.

A chameleon catches a cricket with its long, sticky tongue. Chameleon tongues have been measured to extend 1.5 times the length of the body and are so fast that they can hit the prey in 30 thousands of a second!

Invertebrates and Vertebrates

Biologists, scientists who study living things, divide animals into two large groups: invertebrates and vertebrates.

Vertebrates are animals with backbones. These creatures, including humans, also have internal skeletons.

Most animals, more than 97 percent of all known species, are invertebrates and do not have a backbone. Most invertebrates are insects and live on land. Many invertebrates are aquatic and thus live in rivers, lakes, and oceans. Some invertebrates have evolved with hard shells and exoskeletons that protect them and allow them to move. Other invertebrates have internal skeletons for support.

From Domain to Species

When scientists group animals together, they do this in levels, starting with domains, then kingdoms. Within a kingdom animals are grouped into phyla. Each phylum in turn consists of classes. Each class is made up of orders. Each order is made up of families. Each family contains genuses. Each genus contains species. Each individual type of animal is known as a species. No one knows for sure how many animal species are on the planet, and estimates range from three million to 30 million. The name of a species is given using both the genus and the species name, so in the classification shown below, the scientific name for the lion is *Panthera leo*.

CLASSIFICATION OF THE LION

Domain:	Eukarya	Organisms made up of complex cells
Kingdom:	Animalia	Animals
Phylum:	Chordata	Animals with a supporting, flexible rod down their back
Class:	Mammalia	Animals that have hair and whose females produce milk for their young
Order:	Carnivora	Meat eaters with sharp, pointed teeth
Family:	Felidae	Cats
Genus:	*Panthera*	Large hunting cats such as the lion, tiger, and leopard
Species:	*Panthera leo*	Lions

A lioness with her cubs

Bodies covered with hair

Sharp, pointed teeth adapted to carnivorous diet

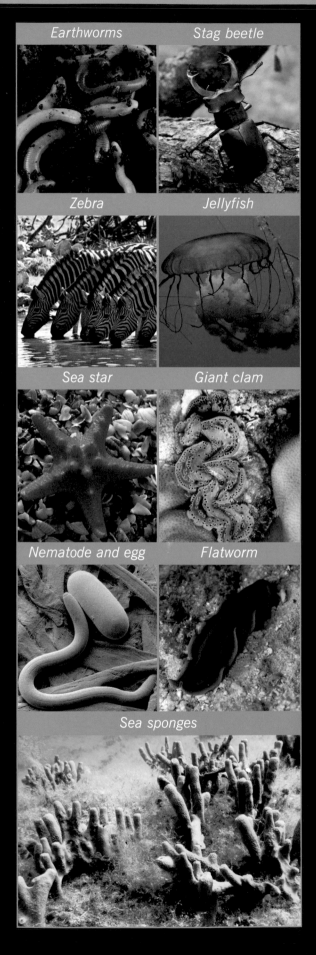

Earthworms

Stag beetle

Zebra

Jellyfish

Sea star

Giant clam

Nematode and egg

Flatworm

Sea sponges

Moving Down a Level in the Animal Kingdom—Phyla

There are 36 different animal phyla. Some consist of just one species. The major phyla include anywhere from 10,000 to more than one million identified species. These include the following:

Phylum Nematoda—roundworms (about 1,000,000 species)

Phylum Annelida—worms made up of multiple segments (16,000+ species)

Phylum Mollusca—mollusks, such as the clam, that have a muscular foot and a round shell (110,000+ species)

Phylum Echinodermata—animals such as starfish and sea stars that have a star-shaped body pattern and spiky spines on the outside of their bodies (about 7,000 species)

Phylum Cnidaria—animals such as corals and jellyfish that have cnidocytes or stinging cells (about 11,000 species)

Phylum Platyhelminthes—flatworms (about 25,000 species)

Phylum Porifera—animals such as sponges that have inner walls with holes in them (9,000+ species)

Phylum Arthropoda—animals such as insects and crabs with a hard outer shell made of chitin (1,000,000+ species)

Phylum Chordata—animals with a long, flexible, rod-like structure along the back. In vertebrates, this structure develops into the backbone. In addition to vertebrates, such as fish, birds, and mammals, chordates include tunicates and lancets, which are invertebrates (100,000+ species)

THE NEWEST PHYLUM

In 1995, scientists discovered tiny creatures living in the mouths of lobsters that didn't fit into any of the known phyla. Their bottle-shaped bodies use a sticky disk at their base to attach to the lobster's mouth. At least three species have been identified, each living on a different lobster species. These small water-dwelling animals are members of the 36th phylum, Cycliophora.

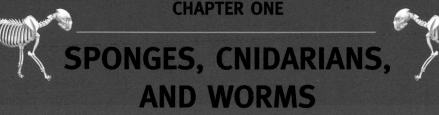

CHAPTER ONE

SPONGES, CNIDARIANS, AND WORMS

S ponges, jellyfish, and worms are all members of the least complex animal phyla. These invertebrates may look very simple, but like all animals, they are specialized, or have adapted, to carry out the necessary functions for life.

Sponges (Porifera): An Ancient Phylum

Sponges make up Porifera (poh-RIF-ur-uh), the simplest and probably the most ancient of all the animal phyla. Most of these animals, which lack organs and nervous or digestive systems, live in the ocean, but there are about 100 freshwater species as well. Sponges are sessile for most of their life cycle, which means that they remain in one spot. In the past, this lack of movement caused them to be mistaken for plants. Two of the features that identify them as members of the kingdom Animalia are the fact that they eat other organisms to stay alive and that they have body parts that work together.

A sponge can have a tiny single sac no more than one-half inch (one centimeter) high, or it can be made of several folded and branching sacs as large as six feet (two meters) high.

Sponges can be shaped like balls, tubes, cups, vases, or fans.

Elephant ear sponge

Home Delivery

When most animals want to eat, they must find food. Sponges wait for their food to come to them in the form of tiny water organisms that are drawn in through the sponge's pores. They are thus known as filter feeders.

The body wall of the sponge has two layers: an outer, skin-like layer and an inner layer lined with collar cells. Collar cells have a long, whip-like projection called a flagellum. The sponge uses these whips to move water through its body. Collar cells also have a sticky surface that traps food, which the sponge then engulfs and digests.

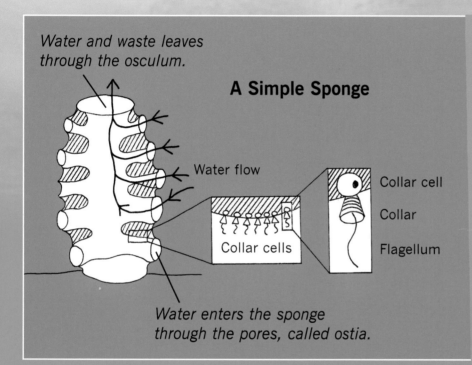

Water and waste leaves through the osculum.

A Simple Sponge

Water flow

Collar cell

Collar

Flagellum

Collar cells

Water enters the sponge through the pores, called ostia.

LEAVE ME ALONE!

Sponges stay in one spot for most of their life cycles, so they are easy prey for animals such as fish, turtles, and sea slugs. Sponges have various methods of protecting themselves against predators. Some can contract, reducing the area exposed to animals that would feed on them. Some give off chemicals that are poisonous or nasty-tasting to their predators. Scientists have begun studying some of these chemicals for possible use in producing medicines.

More of the Same

Cells in the jelly-like layer in the middle of the sponge change into egg cells or sperm cells, but not at the same time in the same sponge. During sexual reproduction, sperm cells are released into the water. When they are taken up by another sponge of the same species they can fertilize that sponge's egg cells. The fertilized eggs develop into new sponge larvae that swim out of the sponge.

Sponges can also reproduce asexually—that is, without needing the cells of two separate organisms to produce offspring. In asexual reproduction, a piece of sponge breaks off and forms a new sponge. This sponge would be identical to the parent sponge.

Sponge larvae leaving the parent animal

The Venus' Flower Basket

The Venus' Flower Basket is a glass sponge living deep on the ocean's floor. Between the two layers of many sponges' bodies is a jelly-like substance that contains slender spikes called spicules. Glass sponges have large spicules that grow together to create a long, tube-shaped glass structure.

Small shrimp enter the sponge by way of its large opening and live inside the sponge, feeding off the food trapped in the sharp strands of the house. As the shrimp get bigger, they can no longer fit through the opening of the sponge, and it becomes their permanent home.

In some cultures, the skeleton of the Venus' Flower Basket is given as a wedding gift. The glass house with shrimp caught inside is thought to represent faithfulness or everlasting love.

VENUS' FLOWER BASKET

Kingdom:	Animalia
Phylum:	Porifera
Class:	Hexactinellida
Order:	Lyssacinosida
Family:	Euplectellidae
Genus:	*Euplectella*
Species:	*Euplectella aspergillum*

A glass sponge skeleton formed by silica spicules

11

Cnidarians (Cnidaria): Radials and Stingers

Like sponges, cnidarians (nih-DARE-ee-uns) are found only in water, and most are found in the ocean. They can spend most of their lives attached to rocks or free-floating in the ocean. Many, such as individual jellyfish and sea anemones, are solitary animals. Others, such as the Portuguese man-of-war, are made up of several tiny individuals that function together as a single creature, while still others, such as corals, form vast colonies.

THE CLASSES OF CNIDARIA		
CLASSES	REPRESENTATIVE ANIMALS	CHARACTERISTICS
Hydrozoa:	Obelia, Portuguese man-of-war	Both polyp and medusa forms in most species
Scyphozoa:	Jellyfish	Medusa is the predominant stage in the life cycle. Many give off light
Cubozoa:	Box jellyfish and sea wasps	Box-shaped medusa stage. Have complex eyes on the fringes of the medusa
Anthozoa:	Anemones and corals	Most occur only as individual polyps or polyps in colonies

Body Like a Wheel

Cnidarians have radial symmetry. This means that when looked at from one end, they display segmented patterns, like spokes of a wheel. Their bodies are sac-shaped with tentacles at the mouth, which is the opening end of the sac.

The cnidarians' body plan comes in two forms: the polyp, which looks like a long stalk with the mouth at the top; and the medusa, which has the mouth and tentacles on the bottom surface and a domed top. Most species have both forms at some point in their life cycle.

Cnidarians are mostly carnivorous. The name *Cnidaria* comes from the stinging cells, called cnidocytes, that these animals use to capture their prey. Found on the outer skin or tentacles, these stinging cells contain thread capsules that release coiled, hollow threads to surround, stick to, or stab and poison their prey. The tentacles pull the food into the animal's large internal cavity, where food is digested.

Jelly Babies

Cnidarians may reproduce asexually or sexually. Asexual reproduction occurs through the budding off or splitting apart of a segment to form a new animal. Sexual reproduction involves eggs released from one animal being fertilized by sperm from another. The larvae then grow into adult animals.

CASE STUDY

Lion's Mane Jellyfish

The lion's mane jellyfish measures about eight feet (2.4 m) across and drags stinging tentacles, some over 100 feet (30 m) long. This creature lives in the cold waters of the Arctic, northern Atlantic, and Pacific oceans. These jellyfish can range from pale orange to dark purple in color. The creature's name comes from the showy and colorful display of its many tentacles.

LION'S MANE JELLYFISH

Kingdom:	Animalia
Phylum:	Cnidaria
Class:	Scyphozoa
Order:	Semaeostomeae
Family:	Cyaneidae
Genus:	Cyanea
Species:	Cyanea capillata

As cnidarians have only one opening, they expel waste products back out of their mouths.

OUT AND ABOUT

Cnidarians don't have brains or nervous cords, but they do have a nerve network with sense organs that detect light. They also lack true muscles, but they do have cells that contract. If the animal closes its mouth and contracts those cells, the rush of water inside its internal cavity can give it the kind of push it needs in order to travel.

Stinging tentacles

Worms: Not Quite Alike

If it's long and skinny and wriggles, but doesn't have a backbone, it's probably some kind of worm. Worms make up three different phyla—flatworms (Platyhelminthes); roundworms (Nematoda); and segmented worms (Annelida). Worms usually live in aquatic or damp environments. They all have bilateral symmetry, which means that if a line is drawn down the middle of one from head to tail, the two sides would be mirror images. Annelids (earthworms and other segmented worms) have the most complex body form with a coelom, or fluid-filled body cavity, within a cell layer. This cavity contains internal organs.

Common earthworm seen under a microscope

The worm uses these tiny chaetae (thorn-like projections) to help it move.

FEED ME!

Worms can be free-living animals, or they can be parasites—animals that live on or in other animals. Flatworms digest their food in individual cells or in a combination of individual cells and a tube-like digestive tract with only one opening. Roundworms and annelids have digestive tracts with both a mouth at one end and an anus at the other. They have more complex digestive systems than flatworms and circulatory systems with blood vessels but no hearts.

Anus

Body segments

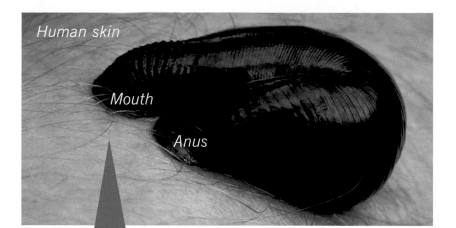

Human skin

Mouth

Anus

MEDICAL LEECHES

Kingdom: Animalia
Phylum: Annelida
Class: Clitellata
Order: Arhynchobdellida
Family: Hirudinidae
Genus: *Hirudo*
Species: *Hirudo medicinalis*

A leech attached by its sucker (mouth) bites through the skin. The body of the leech swells up with blood.

Medical Leeches

CASE STUDY

If you have ever picked up an earthworm and held it in your hand, the gentle creature might have slowly wriggled across your palm. If you picked up a *Hirudo medicinalis*, another species of segmented worm, it would attach itself by going through your skin and would then begin to suck your blood. As gross as a blood-sucking leech might sound, about 15 kinds of these animals are used by surgeons in complicated medical procedures. When doctors have reattached a severed body part, such as a finger or ear, the leeches may be placed on this area of skin to relieve swelling and keep blood flowing. Scientists are also studying leech saliva, which contains natural antibiotics and anesthetics.

Tiny Wrigglers

Sexual reproduction involves the sperm of one worm fertilizing the eggs of another. The eggs are fertilized within the worm and then excreted out the end of the worm. Among the many phyla of worms, only flatworms have true asexual reproduction.

All the phyla of worms can also re-grow some sections of their bodies if they are cut apart. Some can even regenerate an entire body from a part that is missing the worm's head!

Informed Response

All types of worms have a system of nerve fibers to detect the outside environment. Some free-living worms also have eyespots to detect light and movement and cells that detect changes in the chemicals in their environment. Parasitic worms often have less-developed sensory systems. Although all the worms have nerves, only the annelids have what scientists would consider a simple brain.

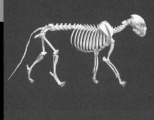
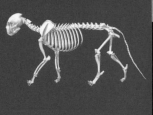
MOLLUSKS AND ECHINODERMS

Like the simpler animals, many of the mollusks and all of the echinoderms are found in or near water. They include some of the most beautiful, colorful, and diverse types of animals. Some of these invertebrates have developed very sophisticated sensory organs, allowing them to interact very successfully with changes in their environments.

Mollusks: Soft and Sessile

The phylum Mollusca gets its name from the Latin word *molluscus*, which means "soft." Mollusks do indeed have soft bodies, which are often protected by a hard shell. These animals are mostly ocean dwellers, although some live in freshwater lakes and others live in moist places on land. Some, including oysters, which attach themselves to the ocean floor, are sessile and thus remain in one place throughout their life cycle. Others, such as squid, which use a type of jet propulsion, can travel quickly.

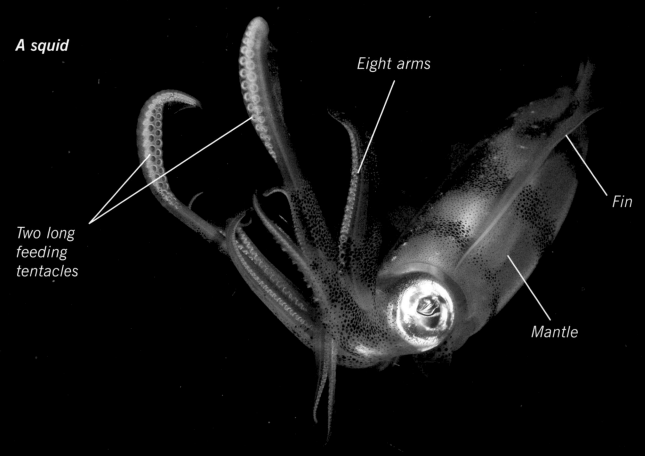

A squid

Eight arms

Fin

Two long feeding tentacles

Mantle

Variations on a Theme

There are seven different classes of mollusks. These animals often bear no resemblance to each other, but they are all variations of the same basic body plan. All of them have a muscular foot used for locomotion or attachment. All mollusks have a group of internal organs called a visceral mass, and they have a structure called a mantle. The mantle is a membrane that surrounds the internal organs, and it is the body part that can secrete or form the animal's shell.

Super Drills

Mollusks have digestive systems with a mouth and an anus. The bulk of their digestive tract is located within the visceral mass along with the animal's coelom, two- or three-chambered heart, reproductive organs, and a kidney used to remove wastes from its blood.

Some mollusks are filter feeders, relying on water currents to whisk food into their shells. Others have developed an unusual rasping, tongue-like organ called a radula that they use to scrape up food.

The "teeth" on a snail's radula (tongue) seen under a microscope

Muscular foot

MAJOR CLASSES OF MOLLUSCA		
CLASSES	**REPRESENTATIVE ANIMALS**	**CHARACTERISTICS**
Gastropoda:	Snails, abalone, limpets, slugs	One-shelled mollusks with a large muscular foot positioned under the animal's body
Bivalvia:	Clams, mussels, oysters, scallops	Two-shelled animals, mostly filter feeders
Cephalopodia:	Octopuses, squid, cuttlefish, chambered nautilus	Marine animals with the foot evolved into tentacles with suckers or hooks. Only the nautilus has an external shell. Move by jet propulsion—squirting water out of a muscular tube

Water Babies

Mollusks reproduce sexually. Most have separate sexes, but some land-dwelling species and a few bivalves (two-shelled mollusks) are hermaphrodites. Aquatic mollusks usually release their eggs and sperm into the water. Fertilization occurs in the water, and the larvae travel and develop into adults in the water. On land, in animals such as snails, internal fertilization is more common. The animals use their reproductive organs to mate. When the eggs are fertilized, the snail squeezes them out and they hatch into young.

Breathing Easy

Mollusks have circulatory systems to move blood within their bodies. The blood moves through the system pumped along by a two- or three-chambered heart. Oxygen that the animal needs goes into the blood, and waste gases go out through either gills or a primitive type of lung. These animals have also evolved disposal structures, a type of primitive kidney, to remove wastes from the blood.

CAN YOU OPEN THIS FOR ME?

The next time you need help opening a bottle, perhaps you can ask an octopus for assistance. Researchers have discovered that the giant Pacific octopus can twist a lid off a bottle to get at its dinner. Initially, it takes about 15 minutes for an octopus to open the jar. With practice, some octopuses can get at their fishy meal within two minutes, using just two of their eight tentacles to remove the top. Not only can they open regular jars and bottles, but with practice they can also open childproof pill bottles in under five minutes!

AMAZING EYES, SKIN, AND MUSCLES

Octopuses have amazing eyes. Most octopuses see their world in black, white, and shades of gray. They can detect certain kinds of light that allow them to see transparent creatures such as jellyfish. They can also detect colors around them in order to change their skin color. In addition, muscles on their skin contract or expand, changing the skin's texture to match surrounding coral, sand, or rocks (as above). The muscles that control an octopus's eye movements are also amazing. They allow its slit-shaped pupil to remain horizontal, even when the creature is balanced sideways or upside down!

Blue-ringed Octopus

What is the size of a golf ball and carries enough venom to kill 26 adults? The colorful blue-ringed octopus, a mollusk found in the warm waters near Australia, is a deadly creature. Most octopuses are shy and harmless. The blue-ringed octopus is also usually quite shy and calm. If stepped on or attacked, however, it will defend itself. It has a razor-sharp beak that can easily cut through a diver's wet suit and inject a poison that will first paralyze and then kill a person within minutes if not treated immediately. There is no known antidote for this venom, but immediate and constant artificial respiration to keep the patient getting oxygen will usually result in recovery.

BLUE-RINGED OCTOPUS

Kingdom:	Animalia
Phylum:	Mollusca
Class:	Cephalopoda
Order:	Octopoda
Family:	Octopodidae
Genus:	*Hapalochlaena*
Species:	*Hapalochlaena maculosa*

Echinoderms: Spiny and Symmetrical

Echinoderms are often shaped like a five-sided star or a wheel with five spokes. The name *echinoderm* comes from the Greek words for "spiny skin," and most of these animals have prickly spikes that keep them free of floating debris. The spikes and plates of their spiny skin are actually under the skin, forming an endoskeleton made of calcium carbonate—the same material found in clamshells.

SOME OF THE MAJOR CLASSES OF ECHINODERMA

CLASSES	REPRESENTATIVE ANIMALS	CHARACTERISTICS
Asteroidea:	Sea stars (also called starfish)	Star-shaped bodies with five to more than 20 arms, mouth on bottom
Echinoidea:	Sea urchins and sand dollars	Spherical or disk-shaped, no arms, complex mouth structure
Holothuroidea:	Sea cucumbers	Soft, cucumber-shaped body

European edible sea urchin

Sea star

Seafood Buffet

Some echinoderms are filter feeders and eat microscopic organisms in the water. Others graze on algae, which they scrape off of rocks on the ocean floor. Some species of sea stars are carnivorous predators that eat crustaceans, worms, mollusks, and other echinoderms. A sea star attaches itself to a clamshell using its tube feet. It pries the shells apart and pushes out its stomach through its mouth on its bottom surface. The stomach enters the mollusk shell, where it digests the body of the mollusk. Then it scoops up the digested bits and is pulled back through the mouth into the sea star.

Mouth

Tube feet

Leather star prey

Common sea star larva

FLUID-FILLED CANALS

Echinoderms have an extensive network of water-filled canals that form a water vascular system. The canals branch into hundreds of tiny tube feet that can move around when filled with water. These animals use this system to travel around, help them eat, and help them breathe by absorbing oxygen. A sunflower sea star has 15,000 tube-like feet and can zoom along the ocean floor at speeds of ten feet (three m) per minute. In this photograph, a morning sun star, aided by its tube feet, is shown feeding on a leather star.

TWINKLE, TWINKLE LITTLE STAR

When echinoderms mate, the separate male and female animals release their sperm and eggs into the water, where the fertilized eggs develop into new animals. Echinoderms are unusual because they have larvae with bilateral symmetry (two matching sides) that become adult forms with radial symmetry (many matching parts).

CHAPTER THREE

ARTHROPODS

Arthropoda is arguably the most successful phylum that has ever existed. There are more than one million species of these animals, and scientists estimate that the arthropod population of the world is about one billion billion individual animals. That is one followed by 18 zeros. Approximately three out of every four animals on the planet are members of this phylum.

An Abundance of Beasts

The phylum's better-known members include insects, arachnids (spiders, scorpions, mites, ticks, and others), and crustaceans (lobsters, crabs, shrimp, crayfish, and others). These invertebrates live everywhere, in all climates, and in a wide range of habitats from the oceans to the deserts.

Animals in Armor

One thing that arthropods have in common is that they have an exoskeleton. They have what is essentially a suit of armor made of protein and a chemical called chitin covering the soft parts of their body. This covering keeps them from drying out so that arthropods can live in both wet and dry areas.

Just like armor, the exoskeleton is segmented, and in between the segments are joints where the animal can bend. These animals have jointed appendages such as legs and antennae that are not found in the simpler animals. Arthropods get their name, which means "jointed feet," from this characteristic.

THE FOUR SUBPHYLA OF ARTHROPODA		
SUBPHYLA	**REPRESENTATIVE ANIMALS**	**CHARACTERISTICS**
Chelicerata:	Spiders, ticks, scorpions, horseshoe crabs	Appendages that act like pincers, four or five pairs of legs, no antennae, some terrestrial and some marine
Myriapoda:	Centipedes, millipedes	Pair of antennae, pair of mandibles, centipedes with one pair of legs per body segment, millipedes with two pairs per body segment
Hexapoda:	Flies, bees, ants	Mainly terrestrial, bodies divided into three parts, three pairs of legs, usually two pairs of wings, antennae; undergoes metamorphosis
Crustacea:	Crabs, lobsters, shrimp, barnacles	Crabs, lobsters, shrimp: marine, travel, two or three body parts, antennae, chewing mouthparts, three or more pairs of legs; Barnacles: marine, sessile

Spider — *Four pairs of legs*

Scorpion — *Four pairs of legs and pincers*

Tick on human skin — *Piercing mouthparts*

Centipede — *Head with antennae*

Millipede — *Two pairs of legs per body segment*

Fly — *Three pairs of legs*

Honeybee — *Two pairs of wings*

Ant — *Body in three parts*

Crab — *Chewing mouthparts*

Lobster — *Five pairs of legs*

Shrimp — *Two pairs of antennae*

Barnacles — *Protective body plates*

Good Food and "Conversation"

Some arthropods, such as ants and bees, use their appendages to help them eat. They also have a diversity of mouthparts that allow them to eat a wide variety of foods. Some, such as the mosquito or the sand fly, draw up blood using needle-like mouthparts. Others, such as moths and butterflies, use long tubes as drinking straws to suck up nectar. Barnacles are filter feeders; flies mop up pre-digested food, known as pap; and locusts chew up leaves. This wide variety of diets and adaptations is one reason these animals are so successful.

Not only do arthropods live everywhere and eat everything, but some arthropod species form very sophisticated colonies and communicate with each other—usually for purposes of mating—using display "dances" and chemicals they give off called pheromones.

Some arthropods grow and change body shape in a process called metamorphosis. Here is the life cycle of a peacock butterfly.

An adult butterfly lays eggs, which develop into larvae—caterpillars.

The caterpillar grows and molts several times.

During the pupa stage, the caterpillar forms a cocoon.

The butterfly (adult) emerges and flies away.

Inside the cocoon, it grows and rearranges its body form.

WOODLOUSE

Kingdom:	Animalia
Phylum:	Arthropoda
Subphylum:	Crustacea
Class:	Malacostraca
Order:	Isopoda
Family:	Oniscidae
Genus:	*Oniscus*
Species:	*Oniscus asellus*

TOBACCO HORNWORM MOTH

Scientists have discovered that moths retain memories of what they sensed as caterpillars. Researchers used mild electric shocks to train tobacco hornworm caterpillars to avoid the smell of a chemical. After developing into full-grown moths, 75 percent of the creatures exposed to the shocks avoided the smell of that chemical. These findings indicate that although the moth looks as if it was rebuilt entirely while undergoing its metamorphosis from larva to adult, parts of its nervous system remain intact. These findings may help "teach" moths and butterflies to avoid certain plants.

Young woodlice emerge from their mother's brood pouch.

Woodlouse: The Household Crustacean

CASE STUDY

Where do you think you would find a crustacean around the house? Perhaps there might be some shrimp, a lobster, or crabs in the refrigerator, but what about live ones roaming around the garden? The woodlouse (also known as the pill bug) is actually a crustacean. Like lobsters, woodlice need to be wet because they breathe through gills. Also like other crustaceans, they have a hard, shell-like exoskeleton, which they shed as they grow. Unlike other crustaceans, females carry their fertilized eggs in a pouch, much like a kangaroo, until they hatch.

CASE STUDY

Horseshoe Crab: Nature's Blood Donor

Despite its name, the horseshoe crab is not related to king crabs or other kinds of crustaceans that humans consume. This creature is a chelicerate and is more closely related to a spider. Horseshoe crabs are carefully harvested each year from waters throughout the state of Delaware. They are taken back to a lab, where up to 30 percent of their blood is drained from their bodies. The crabs are able to withstand this loss with no ill effect. They are then returned to the water.

Unlike human blood, which is red because it is iron-based, the horseshoe crab's blood is blue due to the copper in its system. The blood from these animals is helpful in producing a great number of drugs, vaccines, and medical devices. The blood is used as part of a test to ensure these products are bacteria-free. Not only is their blood useful, but chitin from the crabs has also been used to make specially coated medical supplies for use on burn victims.

A horseshoe crab gives blood at a biotechnology laboratory.

HORSESHOE CRAB

Kingdom:	Animalia
Phylum:	Arthropoda
Subphylum:	Chelicerata
Class:	Merostomata
Order:	Xiphosura
Family:	Limulidae
Genus:	*Limulus*
Species:	*Limulus polyphemus*

SHEDDING THEIR ARMOR

Exoskeletons have advantages for arthropods, but they also have some disadvantages. In order for the arthropods to grow, they have to shed their armor in a process called molting. During molting, the arthropod leaves its body unprotected until the new exoskeleton hardens. Exoskeletons are also heavy, and the larger an animal is, the thicker the exoskeleton must be. This tends to keep arthropods quite small compared to animals in other phyla.

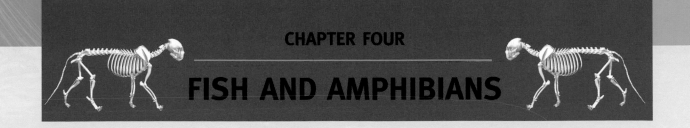

CHAPTER FOUR

FISH AND AMPHIBIANS

Fish and amphibians are both members of the phylum Chordata. The chordates include all of the vertebrate animals. What makes fish and amphibians special is that for some or all of their lives, they live in water.

Fish: Masters of the Deep

The phylum Chordata includes a wide variety of fish. They can be found in nearly every type of aquatic environment. These animals live in freshwater and saltwater, from tiny ponds to enormous oceans. They live in warm tropical waters and in the cold, dark waters under the polar ice caps. Fish have highly developed sensory systems. Not only do they have senses of sight and smell, they also have a series of fluid-filled canals, called a lateral line system, to detect movement.

A salmon

GULF TOADFISH

Most people, if asked to make the sound of an animal, might meow like a cat or chirp like a bird, but could they make the sound of a fish? The male Gulf toadfish makes a grunting sound called the "boatwhistle" to attract females. The sound is somewhat like the noise a toad makes, but does not come from vocal cords. It comes from the fish's swim bladder.

Great Gills

Most fish have gills to breathe. Water washes over the gills and blood circulates through the gills, allowing oxygen from the water to enter the fish's blood. At the same time, carbon dioxide leaves the gills and enters the water. Fish pump blood through their bodies using a closed circulatory system with a two-chambered heart.

Streamlined and Scaled

Olympic swimmers have nothing on these creatures. Fish have evolved to be expert swimmers. They have streamlined bodies with pairs of appendages called fins that they use to maneuver through the water. Fish skin is specially adapted to reduce drag as they move through the water. Most fish have scales, or overlapping plates of skin, that scientists have used to classify the fish into groups and, by counting the yearly growth rings on their scales, estimate the age of certain fish.

Salmon scales *Shark scales*

Fish scales seen under a scanning electron microscope

Classifying Fish

Fish belong to five classes. Two of these classes—Myxini (hagfish) and Cephalaspidomorphi (lampreys)—are jawless, cartilaginous fish. Cartilaginous fish have internal skeletons made from cartilage, the same flexible material that makes up the support for human ears or the ridge on the human nose. The third class, Chondrichthyes, which is made up of cartilaginous fish with jaws, includes sharks, skates, and rays. The final two classes, Sarcopterygii (lobe-finned fish) and Actinopterygii (ray-finned fish) are bony fish. Most of the fish we eat, such as salmon, tuna, and trout, are Actinopterygii.

GOBLIN SHARK

Kingdom:	Animalia
Phylum:	Chordata
Class:	Chondrichthyes
Order:	Lamniformes
Family:	Mitsukurinidae
Genus:	*Mitsukurina*
Species:	*Mitsukurina owstoni*

CASE STUDY

Goblin Shark

The goblin shark, true to its name, looks like a bubble-gum-pink goblin. The shark's skin is semi-transparent, and the rosy hue is caused by blood vessels under the skin. The flattened fins are bluish at the edges and lie close to the body of the shark. The shark's huge jaws are retractable, which means that they can be pushed in and out of the body tissue around the mouth, making this fish look like a creature from a science fiction movie.

A goblin shark found in the ocean around Japan.

Personal Floatation Devices

Fish float at various depths. As they move to different depths, they control their buoyancy in order to control their floating. Sharks do this by storing oil in their livers to give them buoyancy. Even with oil to keep them afloat, they must keep moving or they will sink. Most bony fish have developed an air sac called a swim bladder to allow them to adjust their buoyancy. Gases pass from the animal's blood into the sac to make the fish rise in the water. Transferring the gases back to the blood will make the fish sink.

Creating Schools Of Fish

All fish reproduce sexually. Most bony fish reproduce by external fertilization, in which the eggs and sperm are released into the water. Cartilaginous fish, such as sharks, have internal fertilization. The male uses a pair of appendages called claspers to transfer sperm to the female. Some female sharks release the fertilized eggs at this point, while others develop the eggs internally and give birth to live offspring.

Amphibians: Evolutionary Masterpieces

Amphibians are members of the class Amphibia. They are thought to have evolved from fish. Amphibians have several adaptations that allow them to be successful on land as well as in water.

Moving out of the water and onto the land requires different means of locomotion. Some amphibians crawl close to the ground. Others, such as frogs, leap high into the air. Both of these adaptations require stronger limb bones than those found in fish.

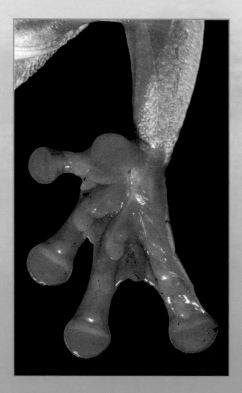

Some species of frogs, such as the red-eyed tree frog, have developed structures like suction cups on their feet that allow them to climb.

ORDERS OF AMPHIBIANS		
ORDERS	**REPRESENTATIVE ANIMALS**	**CHARACTERISTICS**
Anura:	Frogs, toads	No tails, can jump
Caudata:	Salamanders	Long bodies, legs, tails
Gymnophiona:	Caecilians	Adults have no legs and appear worm-like

Living a Double Life

Amphibians live in water for part of their life cycles. For most amphibians, this means that they are hatched in water, where they live as larvae, and move onto land when they become adults. These animals have eggs but, as the eggs have no shell, they can dry out. Most amphibians release their eggs into the water, where they are fertilized, although some species of salamanders have internal fertilization.

Breathing Through Their Skin

Amphibians have an efficient three-chambered heart. Their blood moves through an internal circulatory system and goes into their lungs. The lungs of amphibians are not as well developed as those of other land animals, so they also breathe through their skin. In order for this to happen, the skin must be kept moist, so many amphibians have special glands that secrete slimy mucus. Although amphibians have kidneys that filter waste from their blood, some waste materials also leave their blood directly through their skin.

Some frog species lay their eggs on the underside of leaves above the water, where the eggs will be safe from predators. These eggs are wrapped in a slimy substance that keeps them moist. Once the eggs mature, the larvae, or tadpoles, drop into the water.

Above: Here, the tadpoles of a red-eyed tree frog (inset) are beginning to drop into the water below.

Nerve and Sensory Tools

Like fish, amphibians have well-developed nervous and sensory systems. Many species have not only a lateral line system like fish, but also structures on either side of the head called tympanic membranes that act like eardrums to detect vibrations. They also have well-developed eyes with specialized eyelids, called nictitating membranes, that protect their eyes in water and from drying out in air.

Amphibians can signal each other by making sounds. Some species do this to attract mates, others do it to warn off intruders, and some are even thought to make sounds to give directions to other amphibians.

THE OLM

The olm is a tiny, blind cave amphibian that lives in total darkness in the waters of caves in Europe. It can survive without food for up to ten years. This extremely rare creature is an ancient salamander and is unlike just about any other amphibian. It does not go through metamorphosis.

The adults still have gills and tail fins and do not have eyelids. Despite being blind, the animal's other senses are quite developed, and it can hear and smell.

DISAPPEARING FROM THE PLANET?

Amphibians don't have fur or feathers to protect them. This makes them attractive prey for other animals. One form of protection they have developed is poisonous toxins and bright warning colors and patterns (such as this harlequin poison dart frog above) to tell their predators that they would not be a good food choice. Despite these adaptations, amphibians' numbers are decreasing at an alarming rate. Scientists believe this is due to several factors, including the loss of amphibian habitats, water and air pollution, parasites, viruses, and a type of deadly fungus.

CASE STUDY

Myer's Surinam Toad

The Myer's Surinam toad is an extremely rare animal with a flattened body that makes it appear as if it had been run over by a truck. Of the many features that make this amphibian unique, probably the most unusual is how the toad gives birth. The fertilized eggs are stuck to the female's back, where her skin grows over the embryos. When it is time, the fully developed froglets simply pop off the mom's back and into the water.

MYER'S SURINAM TOAD

Kingdom: Animalia
Phylum: Chordata
Class: Amphibia
Order: Anura
Family: Pipidae
Genus: *Pipa*
Species: *Pipa myersi*

TELLING TOADS FROM FROGS

All toads are frogs, but not all frogs are toads. Toads are a type of frog that has certain characteristics. Toads have shorter bodies and legs than most frogs. They are more likely to have dry, warty skin instead of the smooth, damp skin that most frogs possess. Toads tend to lay their eggs in chains, while most frogs lay their eggs in clusters.

Fertilized eggs

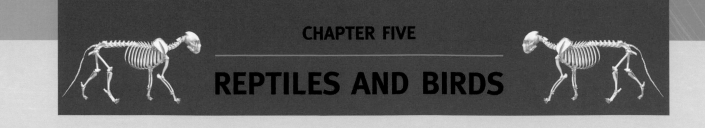

CHAPTER FIVE

REPTILES AND BIRDS

Reptiles and birds are similar animals in many ways. They are both members of the phylum Chordata and have similar bone structures. Where they differ from each other is in how they have adapted to their environments. Reptiles have evolved to be very successful land dwellers. Birds are the most successful vertebrates adapted for life in the air.

Adapted to Water and Land

Like most members of the animal kingdom, reptiles began their development in a watery environment. Also like many groups, they have adapted to live in dry places. In order for their young to fit in with their aquatic environment, the reptiles have developed eggs with a leathery shell and a yolk to nourish the young. Importantly, these eggs also have internal membranes that enclose the fluid inside. Reptile eggs are internally fertilized and usually leave the body of the mother after fertilization, although some snakes and lizards give birth to live young.

Reptiles have several adaptations for life on land. They have scales made of the protein keratin that act as a waterproof barrier, preventing the moisture in their bodies from evaporating. The scales don't grow, so reptiles need to shed their skin, or molt, as they get larger.

Many reptiles are good hunters. Many have eyes that detect color and depth well, and some, such as snakes, have a strong sense of smell.

ORDERS OF REPTILIA

Reptiles, with the exception of snakes,
have well-developed skulls, a backbone
and a tail, two limb girdles (such as
hips and shoulders), and four limbs.

ORDERS	REPRESENTATIVE ANIMALS	CHARACTERISTICS
Squamata:	Lizards, snakes	Scaly, the most plentiful and diverse order
Crocodilia:	Crocodiles, alligators, caimans	Long, broad snout, squat appearance
Testudines:	Turtles, tortoises	Have a shell built into the skeleton
Rhynchocephalia:	Tuatara	Lizard-like reptile found in New Zealand, no external ears, primitive scales

Sun Worshipers

Reptiles are frequently called "cold-blooded" animals, but a more accurate term for them is *ectothermic*. Ectothermic animals use the Sun as their main source of body heat. They may be seen basking in the sunlight on rocks when they are cold and need to warm up. To cool off, they burrow into the soil or sand. Using energy from the Sun rather than chemical energy from food allows reptiles to consume about ten percent less food than similarly sized *endothermic* ("warm-blooded") animals, which must use their own energy to regulate their body temperatures. Being ectothermic, reptiles are better suited to life in tropical and temperate regions than in very cold areas.

Most reptiles have ears with an external membrane connected to a small bone that conducts sound to the detectors in their inner ears.

Snakes rely partly on a sensory organ in the roof of their mouths to find prey. This organ allows them to sample (smell) the air by sticking out their tongues and then touching them to the organ in the roof of their mouths.

Scales

CASE STUDY

Leatherback Turtles

Leatherback sea turtles, the largest of any sea turtles, are turtles without shells. They can grow to be six feet (1.8 meters) long and weigh over one ton (0.9 metric ton). Instead of a hard shell on its back, it has a bony structure under its leather-like skin. These creatures are the fourth-largest living reptiles. In the last 20 years, the eastern Pacific leatherback turtle population has decreased by 90 percent, putting them in grave danger of extinction. They are critically endangered because of a common household item: plastic. Scientists have found fishing lines, balloon bits, spoons, soda can holders, and bags in the stomachs of dead leatherbacks. People can help solve this problem. One way is by cutting down on the use of plastics. Another way is to never release balloons that can then float over the ocean.

LEATHERBACK TURTLE

Kingdom: Animalia
Phylum: Chordata
Class: Reptilia
Order: Testudines
Family: Dermochelyidae
Genus: *Dermochelys*
Species: *Dermochelys coriacea*

A female leatherback turtle comes ashore to lay her eggs on a beach.

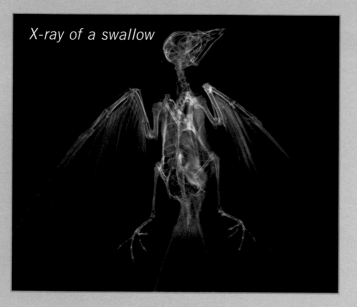

X-ray of a swallow

Birds: Prehistoric Ties

At first glance, a bird and a lizard do not seem to have much in common, but it turns out they are actually quite closely related. Birds evolved from reptiles, and scientists often point out the similarities between the bone structures of modern-day birds and reptiles and those of dinosaurs and other prehistoric reptiles. Birds have kept other characteristics of reptiles as well, such as shelled eggs. The keratin-containing scales of reptiles are still found as scales on birds' legs. Some of these scales have also evolved in birds into toenails and feathers.

Frequent Fliers

Birds, the members of the class Aves, have modifications to the reptile body that enhance flight. Having hollow, honeycombed bones and hollow-shafted feathers reduces the weight of the bird. Other adaptations include large flight muscles and fused bones that better allow the birds to move their wings. The paired limbs that form wings are an airfoil shape that, like the wing of a plane, creates lift and allows the bird to maneuver in the air.

All birds have wings, but there are several species of birds, such as penguins and ostriches, that do not fly. These species are well adapted to living in other environments, such as the water and land.

A swallow in flight

Feathers help birds fly, and they act as a form of insulation, keeping the bird warm and dry. Birds lose their feathers in a process called molting that usually occurs once each year.

Scarlet macaw

Female and male ostrich

Webbed pelican feet

Eagle talons

High Energy

Birds are "warm-blooded," or endothermic, animals. This means that they regulate their internal body temperature, which usually means keeping it above that of their environment. Birds have an average body temperature of about 106 degrees Fahrenheit (41 degrees Celsius). They have a very high metabolic rate, and as a result they need to eat food often. They also need to get oxygen into their bodies quickly. Birds have respiratory systems designed to get oxygen to their lungs both when they inhale and when they exhale.

No Biting Allowed

Having no teeth helps birds keep their body weight down, but it presents challenges to birds that eat hard seeds and insects. These birds have special organs, the crop and the gizzard, that help in the digestive process. When a bird swallows food, the food enters the crop, where it is moistened. The food then passes into the muscular gizzard, where it is rubbed together with small stones the bird has swallowed. Only then does the softened food enter the bird's stomach.

Birds of a Feather Flock Together

There are almost 30 different orders of living birds currently identified. Birds are divided into these orders according to the shape of their skeleton, the shape of their wings, the length of their legs, whether or not they have a gizzard, or even how they lay eggs.

Birds can have bright colors, as do parrots and macaws, to both attract mates and warn enemies to stay away; or long legs, as do flightless emus and ostriches, for out-running predators. They can be adapted for swimming, as are web-footed pelicans, or with sharp talons for hunting, as are raptors such as the eagle.

King Penguin

The king penguin is the second-largest species of penguin. By most standards, this species lives in a very hostile and cold environment. This beautiful creature is now being threatened by global warming. Scientists have observed that when temperatures rise, fewer birds are born, and more of the birds that do hatch are likely to die. The ocean's temperature need only increase by 0.47 degrees Fahrenheit (0.26 degrees Celsius) to have a negative effect on the penguin's survival.

AN UNUSUAL ADAPTATION FOR FLIGHT

Birds have only one ovary, the organ where eggs are formed, and their reproductive organs often shrink in size when they are not breeding. Both these adaptations make the bird's body lighter for flight. Once the birds mate, the fertilized eggs are laid. Most birds incubate their eggs by sitting on them to keep them at a constant temperature. The eggs have a hard outer shell that the chick breaks open at birth. In most species, the parents then provide food for their developing offspring until they are able to feed themselves.

KING PENGUIN

Kingdom:	Animalia
Phylum:	Chordata
Class:	Aves
Order:	Sphenisciformes
Family:	Spheniscidae
Genus:	Aptenodytes
Species:	Aptenodytes patagonicus

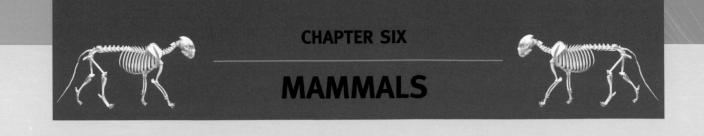
The class Mammalia, which includes humans, is named for the presence of mammary, or milk-producing, glands that are the defining characteristic of these animals. Most mammals give birth to live young and parent their young, with the females feeding them milk until they are able to consume other foods.

High Maintenance

Mammals are all endotherms ("warm-blooded"). They have a high metabolic rate and need to eat about ten times as much as a reptile the same size. To stay warm, they have body hair and a layer of fat under their skin. When it becomes very warm, many mammals sweat, and the evaporation of the sweat cools them down. Some mammals, such as dogs, lack sweat glands, so they pant through their mouths to cool off. Mammals are unusual among the various animal groups because they can have sweat glands, sebaceous or oil-producing glands, and scent glands.

A humpback whale and calf

Deep-Sea Diving

Mammals all use their lungs to breathe air. Marine mammals, known as sirenians (manatees and dugongs) and cetaceans (whales and dolphins), have adaptations that allow them to spend most of their time under water. A typical dive for a sperm whale without needing to come up for air may be an hour. They are able to do this because they can store more oxygen in their body tissues than land mammals, most of which can only hold their breath for several minutes before needing more air.

Got Milk?

Mammals all reproduce sexually with internal fertilization. Once fertilization occurs, the fertilized egg may develop in one of three different ways. Members of the order Monotremata lay their eggs and wait for them to hatch. The monotremes make up a small order that includes the duckbill platypus and two species of echidnas (spiny anteaters) found in Australia and New Guinea.

Marsupials, which include kangaroos, koalas, and wombats, all have pouches. Marsupials bear live young, but the baby finishes developing in its mother's pouch until it is developed enough to emerge.

Most mammals, including humans, are placental mammals. This means that their young develop until birth attached to a placenta—an organ that gives them nourishment from the mother's circulatory system and removes waste. Following the baby's birth, the placenta is expelled from the mother's body. All female species of mammals have mammary glands that produce milk for their young.

A western lowland gorilla nurses her baby.

A kangaroo joey inside its mother's pouch

41

What's for Dinner?

Some mammals are herbivores, which means that they only eat plant material. Herbivores include giraffes, rabbits, and cows. Cats and some other mammals are carnivores, which means that they eat meat. Humans and bears are omnivores, which means that they eat both meat and plant material. Certain species of marine mammals—such as baleen whales and some seals—are filter feeders, straining plankton and small animals from the ocean.

Most mammals have jaws and teeth that are specially adapted to break down their food. Scientists use tooth shape to help classify mammals.

Getting There from Here

Mammals live in a wide variety of habitats. The limbs of many mammals have adaptations for movement. Climbing mammals, such as monkeys, have long, flexible fingers and toes. Mammals that run, such as horses and antelopes, have long, strong limbs. Digging mammals, which include moles, have short limbs with strong claws. Marine mammals have forearms that form large, flat paddles.

FLYING MAMMALS

Bats, which are members of the order Chiroptera, are the only mammals that fly. They have long fingers that support thin flaps of skin, forming wings. Bats also use sound to maneuver while flying and to locate their prey. Using echolocation, the bat gives off a high-pitched sound that bounces off of nearby objects, which the bat can then detect.

CONSTANTLY TEETHING

Almost two-fifths of all mammal species are rodents. This group, which includes rats (as seen here), mice, guinea pigs, porcupines, and chipmunks, have long, sharp front teeth that keep growing throughout the animal's life. Rodents have to keep these teeth from growing too long by gnawing on wood or other plant material.

CASE STUDY

The Problem Solvers

Mammals have nervous systems with brains that direct their bodies' activities. One group, the primates, has developed brains that are large for the size of animals. These highly developed brains make primates excellent problem solvers. They can learn from their environment and alter their behavior so they are more successful. Primates include lemurs, monkeys, apes, and humans. Compared to other mammals—and even to most other primates—humans are not very strong or fast, and they don't have protective fangs or claws, but they are very good at communicating and solving problems because of their large brains.

Just as human babies rely on their parents to learn, orangutans must learn everything they need to know from their mothers. Here, young orangutans orphaned by the cutting down of their rainforest home are taught to find food and be independent by a human worker at an orangutan rescue center.

HUMANS

Kingdom:	Animalia
Phylum:	Chordata
Class:	Mammalia
Order:	Primates
Family:	Hominidae
Genus:	*Homo*
Species:	*Homo sapiens*

Glossary

anesthetics Substances that cause insensitivity to pain

antibiotics Medicines that reduce, inhibit, or destroy bacteria and other microorganisms

bilateral symmetry A body arrangement consisting of two sides that are mirror images of each other

buoyancy The ability or tendency to float in air, water, or some other liquid

carnivorous Feeding on animals

cell The smallest structural or functioning unit of an organism, usually, but not always, consisting of cytoplasm, or protoplasm, and a nucleus surrounded by a membrane

coelom A body cavity of an organism, often between the intestines and the inner wall of the body, containing internal organs

crop A part of the digestive system of birds where food is stored before digestion

echolocation The use of reflected sound signals to detect objects

ectothermic "Cold-blooded"; used to describe animals that don't make their own body heat

endoskeleton The internal supporting structure in animals

endothermic "Warm-blooded"; used to describe animals that use their metabolism to generate body heat

evolve To develop over repeated generations, usually as a way of adapting to changing conditions in the environment

exoskeleton A rigid covering on the outside of some invertebrates, providing protection and support for the body

flagellum A whip-like part of a body or cell

genetic Relating to the passing on of inherited characteristics of an organism

gizzard A part of the digestive system of birds where food is ground into smaller parts

hermaphrodite An organism with both male and female sexual organs

larva The immature form of an animal that changes to become an adult

mantle The membrane that surrounds the internal organs of mollusks

medusa An umbrella-shaped cnidarian body form with a mouth on the bottom surface

metabolic Having to do with the use of energy and the processes that occur within an organism to sustain life

molting Shedding the skin, exoskeleton, or feathers of animals as they grow

mucus A slimy substance secreted by mucus membranes or glands usually in order to protect or lubricate parts of an organism

offspring The young produced by a mature organism

organism An individual animal, plant, or other life form

osculum The opening of a sponge through which water passes

ovary The organ where eggs are produced

pheromone A chemical released by animals that acts to send signals to or affect the behavior of other animals

placenta The organ that connects immature mammals to their mothers and helps give them nourishment before birth

plankton A small or microscopic organism drifting and floating in water. Many animals feed on plankton, primarily by filtering them out of the water

polyp A tube-shaped cnidarian body form, usually with a mouth surrounded by tentacles

radula A structure found in the mouth of certain mollusks that is used to tear food

sessile Attached to one location, immobile

species A group of similar organisms that are capable of exchanging genetic material and breeding; the most individualized classification of a living organism, usually following the group genus and including the name of the genus in its full scientific name

sperm The male sex cell of an organism, usually capable of fertilizing a female sex cell, or egg

spicule A small, hard, needle-like structure found in sponges

swim bladder A gas-filled sac in the body cavity of bony fish that allows them to control their buoyancy

terrestrial Living on, in, or growing from land

tissue A group of specialized cells that work together and form the material out of which a living organism is made

tube feet The numerous body projections of echinoderms that are used to move and secure food

tympanic membrane A thin flap of tissue that vibrates in response to sound; an eardrum

water vascular system The fluid-filled system that allows echinoderms to move

Further Information

animal.discovery.com/

The Discovery Channel Web site has terrific animal videos and current information presented in a child-friendly way.

kids.nationalgeographic.com

This site includes amazing animal photographs and fascinating articles about animals all over the planet from National Geographic.

www.bbc.co.uk/cbbc/wild

A lot of fun facts about animals in captivity and in the wild are on the BBC TV Web site.

www.newscientist.com/

Articles and video clips from *New Scientist* magazine highlight some of the coolest new scientific discoveries.

animaldiversity.ummz.umich.edu

The University of Michigan Department of Zoology Web site has a lot of short articles that are relatively easy to read and filled with good scientific information.

www.nature.com

The latest scientific research and discoveries from the Web site of *Nature* scientific journal.

www.edgeofexistence.org

Amazing photographs and up-to-date information about Evolutionarily Distinct and Globally Endangered (EDGE) animals. The Web site also gives information about what you can do to aid in saving endangered species.

www.tolweb.org

If you are looking for information about the most current taxonomy (classification) of animal species, you will find it here at the Tree of Life Web Project.

www.sciencedaily.com/news/plants_animals

For your daily dose of the latest in scientific discoveries related to animals, check out the images, articles, and video clips on the Science Daily site.

www.sararegistry.gc.ca

To learn more about animals at risk in Canada, you can check out the Species at Risk Public Registry, which includes news, information, and documents on this topic.

www.eol.org

The Encyclopedia of Life Web site contains photographs and scientific information about a wide variety of animals. Just type in the name of the animal you want to see!

www.naturecanada.ca

Numerous articles and links related to nature in Canada. Includes links to Canadian wildlife conservation organizations.

Index

Index

ABOUT THE AUTHORS

Shar Levine and Leslie Johnstone are internationally award-winning, best-selling authors of children's science books and science toys/kits. Leslie Johnstone is also the head of a high school science department. They have written over 50 books and together won the prestigious 2006 Eve Savory Award for Science Communication. Two of their books, *Backyard Science* and *The Ultimate Guide to Your Microscope*, were short-listed for the Subaru Prize for hands-on science activity books. Their Web site is www.sciencelady.com, and Shar's blog can also be found on the Web site.